MW01043015

FIRST IMPRESSIONS

FIRST IMPRESSIONS

Andrew Wyeth

RICHARD MERYMAN

Harry N. Abrams, Inc., Publishers, New York

Series Editor: Robert Morton

Editor: Ellyn Childs Allison

Designer: Jody Hanson

Library of Congress Cataloging-in-Publication Data

Meryman, Richard, 1926-
    Andrew Wyeth / Richard Meryman.
       p.   cm.—(An Abrams first impressions book)
    Summary: Examines the life and work of the popular American artist.
    ISBN 0-8109-3956-8
    1. Wyeth, Andrew, 1917—Juvenile literature.   2. Painters—United States—
Bibliography—Juvenile literature.   [1. Wyeth, Andrew, 1917-.   2. Artists.   3. Painting,
American.   4. Painting, Modern—20th century.   5. Art appreciation.]   I. Title.
II. Series.
ND237.W93M44   1991
759.13—dc20
[B]
[92]   90-47605

Text copyright © 1991 Richard Meryman

Illustrations copyright © 1991 Harry N. Abrams, Inc.

Published in 1991 by Harry N. Abrams, Incorporated, New York
A Times Mirror Company
All rights reserved. No part of the contents of this book may be reproduced without the
written permission of the publisher.

Printed and bound in Hong Kong

Study for **Pine Baron.** 1976
An early sketch that became an important tempera (page 30).

Title page: **Winter Corn.** 1948
Wyeth once said: "When I walk through the rows of blowing corn I'm reminded of the
way a king must have felt walking down the long line of knights on horseback with
banners blowing."

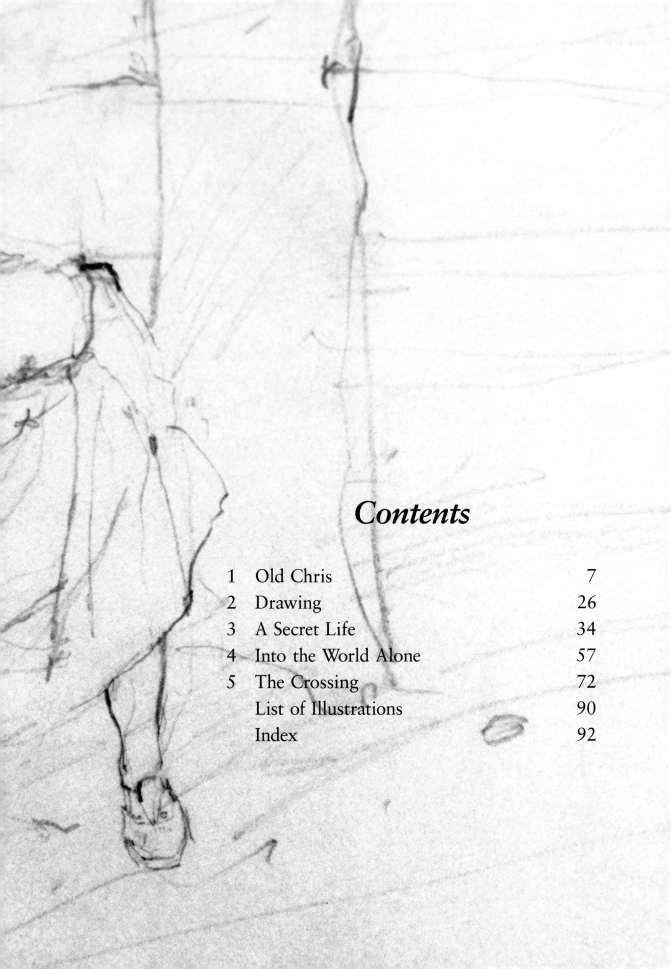

Contents

1
Old Chris

Through all of Andrew Wyeth's life, Halloween has been like a dark Sabbath—"the eerie feeling of another world," he says. "Spirits. Goblins. Witchcraft. Shadows. Dark holes behind windows, a glint of metal in the moonlight—the unreal." Each year he spends hours on an elaborate, often horrific, disguise—a dead-white Dracula, a hairy werewolf. Then, feeling invisible behind his mask of makeup, he leads costumed friends and family through the night, "haunting" his hometown of Chadds Ford, Pennsylvania.

The Halloween ritual is the essence of Andrew Wyeth. Fueled by excitement, by that imagination that burns highest in the child, he is galvanized by terror, the hottest of those thrills. His impish, boyish personality is a mask hiding a solitary seriousness—which masks the powerful emotions he hides in his paintings. And these emotions are masks for a constant torrent of memory—which covers what nobody can guess. He is a gallery of magic mirrors—crafty, brave, warm, shocking, ruthless, generous, obsessed.

Wyeth paints recognizable objects—hills, cornstalks, houses, spruce trees, animals, and country men, women, girls, boys going about their lives. Viewers who do not see beyond the surface reality think he is recording a vanishing rural America.

Jack Be Nimble. 1976
Wyeth's boyhood fascination with witchcraft and the delicious
terrors of the night live in his painting of a stack of Halloween
pumpkins he carved himself.

For an annual family Halloween "haunt," Wyeth made up as an Indian scout for George Washington and wore a Continental Army coat. His mother tried to guess who wore each disguise.

They are absolutely wrong. "People who don't look at my work," Wyeth says angrily, "think I'm a painter of old oaken buckets. I'm *anything* but that!"

Wyeth follows the centuries-long tradition of realistic painting, from Albrecht Dürer through Rembrandt to Thomas Eakins and Winslow Homer. But he is also

Wolf Moon. 1975

Looking at the artist's view of the moonlit Kuerner's farm in the snow right side up and upside down shows Wyeth's combination of abstract pattern and realistic detail.

in tune with today's abstract artists, who regard the surface skin of reality as a sort of static that jams deeper truths. They obliterate recognizable images and create their own versions of reality that directly express their feelings. In his major works, Wyeth's luminous images are austere, reserved, eerie—ghosts of the reality. But pulsing subtly behind those withdrawn surfaces is violence and anger, love, hurt, and fear. Like the abstractionists, he hopes that viewers will sense the emotions that wrack him and find their own strong feelings.

He, too, alters reality. A painting is never the same as the scene. In a composition, sizes and arrangements of objects are altered for effect. In one picture, *Her Room,* which shows the living room in his Cushing, Maine, house, he has left out

Her Room. 1963

One windy day in Maine, while worried about his son out in a boat, Wyeth was startled as the living room door blew open with a bang and an eerie light fell on the rough sea.

N.C. Wyeth. **Siege of the Round House.** 1913

Wyeth's father painted this scene for a new edition of Robert Louis
Stevenson's novel *Kidnapped* in 1913. The action seems to explode
on the page, and Wyeth marvels that his father achieved such
dramatic motion and drew so accurately from his imagination.
"Look at those teeth," he has said, "you just see the teeth of a
cornered rat. I know that was on my father's mind."

all furniture—a sofa, tables, lamps—except a chest. Almost imperceptibly, the lines of the door, windows, and chest are skewed, helping to create subliminal terror, a sense of tragedy happening beyond this sunlit silence.

Wyeth considers himself an abstractionist expressing emotions *through* reality—feelings so powerful they might crack his sanity if he did not paint them. Sometimes, when he cannot transmit his passion to the flat surface, "I tear pictures right in two trying to get into them," he says.

Everything that shaped Andrew Wyeth as a painter happened between his birth on July 12, 1917, and 1945, when he was twenty-eight. The permeating force that affected almost every corner of his life was his father. Newell Convers Wyeth—known as NC—was the most famous illustrator of his day, celebrated for his classic illustrations for such books as *Kidnapped, Treasure Island, The Black Arrow,* and *The Merry Adventures of Robin Hood.* In NC's world of ferocious drama, massive men with bulging calves and mighty biceps drew longbows, slashed with cutlasses, galloped horses. Gun butts glinted. Glittering teeth gripped a knife—or clenched like a cornered rat's. Dangerous eyes gleamed in menacing faces. Moonlight rimmed a hand with fear. Blood stained a hand with death.

N. C. Wyeth could have been the creation of his own explosive imagination. He was 6 feet 2 inches tall, weighed 240 pounds, had broad shoulders, a barrel chest, narrow hips. He had the raw strength to lift a friend's Model-T Ford free of a mud hole. He wore his hair long and usually had on a western-style wide-brimmed, high-crowned hat and knickers. One of his students and later son-in-law, Peter Hurd, a famous southwestern artist, said, "He looked like a Brahma bull—tapered down to fine legs, fine ankles. Light on his feet, walked with a bounce."

NC was capable of direct, unflinching action that bordered on the brutal. During four months he spent in the Southwest in 1904, he was working as a cowboy. A horse died during a roundup. With a knife he cut it up to study its anatomy. When a dog had to be put away, he took it to the woods and fired a bullet

In this family photograph made in 1923, N.C. Wyeth dominated, as he did in real life. Left to right are: Ann, Carolyn, Mrs. N.C. Wyeth, Andrew, Nathaniel, and Henriette.

N.C. Wyeth. **Portrait of My Mother.** 1929
Wyeth's father painted this portrait of his mother in Needham, Massachusetts, where the family lived.

into its head. When a rabbit hunter ignored a request to leave the property, NC threw him and his shotgun over the fence into the brambles. When he was driving his new wife, Carolyn, in a rented horse and buggy, the horse balked at a railroad crossing. To make the horse cross the tracks, NC beat its head bloody with the reins.

Though NC's voice was high, from his huge chest could come a bellow that carried a mile down the small valley of the Brandywine River, summoning his children home from skating on an upriver slough. Sometimes when the train whistle echoed from the crossing, the Wyeth children answered it, thinking it was NC. "I came from a father," says Andrew Wyeth, "who was blood and guts."

An opposite side of NC was deeply poetic, able to write about a Maine harbor: "The water lies like molten glass that has cooled, its glint slightly dulled by a faint trace of dust—sky dust." Sometimes his illustrations switched gears into pastoral serenity, a delicate tenderness. He was passionate about all sides of life, especially the arts. He read avidly—Henry David Thoreau, Leo Tolstoi, Robert Frost—and talked to the children about Shakespeare while giving them castor oil. A passable

pianist able to play the easier classics, he listened to Bach and Beethoven on the tall windup Victrola, head bowed close to the open loudspeaker door, hand over his eyes, the family afraid to make a sound. "He lowered himself into music as if going slowly into water," says his eldest daughter, Henriette. In later years, Andrew's aunt Elizabeth Sargent believed, "You feel that music in Andy's paintings— intonations—spacing. I think sometimes when he paints, he's hearing something."

According to family lore, the delicacy in NC's nature came from his French-Swiss grandfather, Jean Denys Zirngiebel, a horticulturist. The Teutonic harshness, which seriously complicated Andrew's relationship with his father, was inherited from his German-Swiss grandmother, named Henriette. Emigrating to

America to help run the Harvard University Botanical Gardens, in Cambridge, Massachusetts, Zirngiebel settled in Needham, thirteen miles west of Boston. Their daughter, also Henriette, married Andrew Newell Wyeth from an old, proud Cambridge family. The young couple lived near her parents and two Zirngiebel brothers. Into this tiny but intensely Swiss community, Newell Convers Wyeth was born in 1882.

He came to Chadds Ford, Pennsylvania, in 1902 to study under the great illustrator and writer Howard Pyle. In 1906 he married Carolyn Bockius, who was from nearby Wilmington, Delaware. She was dark-haired, slender, and very beautiful, a gentle, shy, uncomplicated, uncertain woman who loved baking and took immense pride in her house, family, and possessions. Completely submissive to her husband, she was affectionate and permissive with her children. Andrew always gave his mother a present on *his* birthday. Her granddaughter Ann Carol Hurd says, "Grandma Wyeth was vital, fresh, enfusing—like spring. She was unqualified love. NC was qualified love."

On a hillside they built a small, rectangular, two-story brick and white clapboard house. Fifty yards up the hill he constructed a huge studio. Eventually, with increased prosperity, NC added a wing to the house. NC's property—"this little corner of the world wherein I shall work out my destiny"—overlooked gentle hills patched with forests and fields. Below them, the frame buildings of the small town clustered at the intersection of two tar roads, and the Brandywine River eased through the valley.

Andrew was the youngest of five children, all potent talents and personalities commanding equal attention. Henriette, ten years older than Andrew, was considered the family prodigy. She read at age five, and went through the entire Bible at eight. By ten, she spoke elementary French. A precocious artist, she studied art alone in Boston at age thirteen. At fifteen, beginning a distinguished career, she was doing her own portrait commissions. The next daughter, Carolyn, though tender and vulnerable at center, was the family rebel, indifferent to appearances

As a little boy, Andrew was an imp, full of mischief. Those who know him find that the same face, filled with the devil and with charm, still appears on the man—the excited energy of a child still vitally alive within him and his paintings.

N.C. Wyeth. **Andy with Fire Engine.** 1923

When Andrew posed, his hands were so restless that his father could not paint them and they were left unfinished.

and convention, passionately devoted to animals. She too became an important painter. After a failed marriage, she returned home to live permanently in the family house.

Nathaniel, the next in line, was a born scientist, a boyhood builder of superb ship models and toy speedboats powered by alarm-clock motors. He became a top development engineer for the Du Pont Company. He held dozens of patents for chemical-manufacturing equipment and invented the plastic bottle in which soft drinks are sold today. Ann, two years older than Andrew, lay in bed at age two and hummed Beethoven melodies. She became a composer, and one of her symphonies was played by the Philadelphia Orchestra, directed by Leopold Stokowski. She married a student of NC's named John McCoy, a fine landscape and portrait painter, and settled a few miles from home.

At age two, Andrew could sing the French national anthem, *La Marseillaise*. The first time NC heard that, he wept. Andrew grew into a feverishly hypersensitive child, his mind always at full throttle. He was angelic-looking, with curly blond hair, but an impish glint lit the blue eyes. His father, who referred to "Andy's incessant aliveness," had trouble painting him because his hands were never still. When his father came in the room, Andrew would break into a roguish smile and NC would say, "Andy, stop being foolish."

According to his Aunt Elizabeth, "Andy was a little rascal." At church in Chadds Ford, he hid behind the curtain by the christening font. During the minister's sermon, he stuck his face out between the curtains and made a face at the congregation. Stealing a candy bar at the drugstore, he made Aunt Elizabeth's daughter, Mary Sargent, be the lookout. When she protested, he slipped the candy into *her* pocket and ran out of the store laughing. At a party at the house, he locked the bathroom doors and put Ex-Lax into the punch.

But everybody found Andrew fascinating. In Henriette's memory, "Andy was born with an exquisite, almost painful, sensitivity to life. There was always something inside. You felt he was seeing things only he could see." Aunt Elizabeth once said, "You could see Andy's imagination in his eyes—faraway."

Despite his nervous energy, Andrew's health was delicate. His body was thin. "Food didn't seem to nourish him," Henriette remembers. He suffered from constant sinus trouble. The local doctor treated it with drainage tubes painfully threaded into his sinus passages. Years later, scars of undiagnosed tuberculosis were found on his lungs.

Always it was his father, a warm, surrounding presence, who nursed him. When Andrew had bouts of high fever, his father slept beside him in Nat's bed. At age four, every morning Andrew dutifully stood on a towel in front of his father seated on a chest. NC's beautiful, tapered fingers moved over the skinny body, rubbing olive oil into the pale skin. "It gave Pa a feeling of doing something," Henriette says. "He was a big Nanny. There wasn't one phase of our lives he didn't enter."

NC, devoted to his loving and powerful mother, had mystical feelings for his own household. He once wrote, "How rare is the spirit of family reverence—almost a lost art to many. What an oasis in the desert when one *does* happen upon a person who feels the deeper significance of life—of *family* life." He was determined to fulfill this ideal. "Our world was us," Henriette remembers, "a world of music and countryside and reading and what we were told to do. Heavenly."

NC cooked the breakfast early each morning, banging the pans, grinding the coffee, rousing the whole house. He oversaw the help, checked the groceries, did much of the shopping. He joined the children in play, helping them build dams in the brook down in the woods. He made little paddle wheels from twigs and leaves. He made boats from skunk-cabbage leaves and tiny passengers from flower blossoms. He organized family walks and picnics, found the

For this photograph Andrew posed as the evil Mr. Hyde.

boggy mats of wet leaves where the first spring beauties bloomed. "He wouldn't let you touch them," Henriette remembers. "They were the Holy Grail, as far as we were concerned."

At night NC hovered over the children, making certain they cleaned their plates and ate their crusts. In the evening as he sat reading in a large winged-back chair, one of the children would give him a drawing pad and pencil and ask for a giant, or a Russian, or brownies. Others would hang over the pad as he swiftly drew a giant that picked up a child and, remembered Nat, "did everything but eat it." Once he drew "Old Chris"—his name for Santa Claus—taking a bath with brownies climbing up on ladders to soap him and slide down his back.

He told the children sagas of adventure and derring-do, of spooks and monsters—read to them about Dracula and Dr. Jekyll, who drank a potion and became the homicidal monster Mr. Hyde. "Our nerve ends were vibrating,"

Spring Beauty. 1943

Walking the fields and woods of Chadds Ford, Wyeth has been
tuned to every detail of nature. To the extent that works reveal the
artist who created them, each painting is a portrait of Wyeth's
complexity. In this tempera, a delicate blossom contrasts with the
massive roots, creating a dramatic tension that is also found in
N.C. Wyeth's work.

remembers Ann—and Andrew would be laughing with delicious hysteria. Even a retelling of *Treasure Island* was heart stopping in NC's mouth as he mimicked all the pirate voices. "He *was* those people," remembers Ann. Often at night an over-stimulated Andrew had nightmares or lay awake.

Aunt Elizabeth, a storyteller whose imagination was almost as active as Andrew's, has said, "Andy's father was really himself a character out of Robert Louis Stevenson. He captivated Andy every minute. He was everything that would fire up a child." Wyeth himself says, "It was the most imaginative, rich childhood you could ever want. That's why I have so much inside of me that I want to paint."

Halloween, the Fourth of July, and Christmas were orgies of stimulation. NC announced the Fourth at dawn by throwing a lighted cherry bomb out of an upstairs window. There were firecrackers all day long. Once when they went for a drive, Andrew in the backseat threw a lit pack of firecrackers under the front seat.

Halloween was a mood that filled the house. When the wind rattled in the doorjambs, NC's eyes rolled and his face filled with fright as he told the children, "It's the witches." Ann remembers, "They were *there!* Definitely!"

Christmas Day was the pinnacle of excitement. NC "became" Old Chris in order, as he put it, to "trace fascinating, mystic patterns" on the minds of his children. In the darkness of 5 A.M., dressed in a different costume every year—maybe a fur Eskimo outfit with a pointed cap and huge white eyebrows—he climbed to the ridge of the roof, stamping, ringing sleigh bells, making the sound of a great bag being dragged to the chimney, calling to the reindeer. The house seemed to shake and then came alive with a turmoil of children—"like a fuse running through the house," Ann says. Then Old Chris would come stamping up the stair to shake the hands of the children, just for a fearful second.

Andrew Wyeth says, "I was so excited in the night, I used to wet my bed—and then move to the other side of the bed to let it dry out. I was horrified that Old Chris was going to come up in my room and I'd crawl down under my bedclothes and lie there shaking. I'd hear these heavy steps coming up, and hold my breath till my eyes

Above: Study for **Witch's Broom**. 1984

In Maine, pine trees suffer a blight that kills the limbs in a section of trunk, leaving a tuft at the top like a huge witch's broom turned upside down—an image full of the New England witchcraft that races Wyeth's imagination. In this watercolor sketch he inserted terrifying witch's eyes, and six years later he painted this fantasy in a tempera by the same name.

Opposite: **Sunday Times**. 1987

A newspaper blowing over the damp spring ground and melting snow, brought to Wyeth's mind the happy excitement of Christmases past, when he and his sister played in the snow with colorful wrapping papers in the wind.

would pop out. Old Chris was to me a giant plus a marvelous merry spirit—but a man who was horrifying. Magic."

Wyeth continues, "Of course, I don't think anything is really magical unless it has a terrifying quality. Anything that's *good* is terrifying—and sad. Christmas is joyful, sad, terrifying. I was sad it was over—and glad it was over. I still have the same feeling about Christmas."

In the predawn darkness, with Andrew in the lead, the children filed down the stairs and entered the "big room." The burning logs in the fireplace lit the beams in the ceiling of the long, low room, lit the mural of three nudes by Henriette, the wreaths in the windows along each wall, the baby grand piano in the left corner. The Christmas tree was in the far right corner, real candles burning on its rich green boughs. Behind it in the deep windowsill was the bust of Beethoven. Under it were the unwrapped special presents—a model farm for Carolyn, a bike for Ann. One year, there was a castle made by Nat for Andrew and painted by NC.

Indian Summer. 1970

In the year that his old friend Christina Olson died, Wyeth met a fourteen-year-old Finnish girl named Siri Erickson. The subject of many drawings and paintings, Christina stood for the tough Maine spirit burning in a disintegrating body. Siri's flowering youth, vigorous and unselfconscious, suggested rebirth and he began his first series of paintings of the nude.

Trained by their father, the children stood quietly in a moment of rapture. He was like an orchestra conductor, telling them to savor each moment, take their time, look at the lights, make everything count—be careful when you open your presents because your mother took a long time wrapping them.

Andrew always received soldiers, boxes of them bought by his mother. Ann received dolls—and felt sorry for older Henriette who got stockings or a book. "Pathetic," she would think. Finally, all presents were opened and the floor was deep in brilliant paper. Through the windows, dawn was flowing into the small valley. A thin snow dusted the tawny fields. A faraway dog barked in the quiet. Gallagher's store and the Chadds Ford Hotel grew visible in the tiny village.

The living room was given over to Christmas for weeks. Andrew and Ann piled presents under the tree again and reenacted Christmas. They took long ribbons of wrapping paper out on the hill and let the wind blow them along the ground—"like a dragon," remembers Ann. "It would run after us and wrap around our legs. Scary." Years later, one snowy day, Wyeth was on that hill when a piece of newspaper blew past and he put his foot on it—and "it shivered there for a moment." He drew the paper—and the Christmas dragons—in a rapid watercolor.

Andrew and Ann would come in from sledding outside in the cold and lie under the tree, surrounded by their new toys and gazing into the green, glittering enchantment. The air was rich with the smell of pitch and pine, of new presents and hot wax. One ornament that Andrew watched as it twirled in the updraft from the candles was a German angel made of wax, with tiny wings, one foot melted by a candle. That decoration came to life more than three decades later in Maine, when Wyeth was painting a Finnish teenager named Siri Erickson, who posed for a series of nudes, the first of his career. One shows Siri standing on a veined granite ledge in the Indian summer sun, a spruce tree strong behind her. "Whether or not she was a beauty," Wyeth says, "had nothing to do with my painting her. That husky little figure standing looking off, with the pale blond hair, is the figure of that little angel against the Christmas tree."

The Big Room. 1988

Andrew's sister Carolyn, who lives in their father's house, does not
use the living room. It was the center of their childhood, where the
Christmas tree stood in front of the bust of Beethoven, where
Andrew spread out his soldiers, and where their mother customarily
kept a bowl of apples.

2
Drawing

Within young Andrew, the boundary line between his real and his fantasy life barely existed. The world of imagination, the vast and flowing story he was constructing, was as immediate, as vital, as any daily fact. All day long everything nourished and mingled his make-believe. "I always had a reason to draw," Wyeth remembers.

Andrew did not suffer the force-fed reality of school. NC believed that good artists never come from classrooms—and Andrew was judged too sensitive and nervous for that rough-and-tumble. So he was tutored at home at a table in the basement playroom by a local girl named Lydia Betts. During the lessons, he kept glancing back at his hundreds of toy World War I soldiers on shelves behind him. "They were real little people to me," Wyeth says. "I could see the smirk on their painted faces. A worn place looked like a moustache, or a wound on the side."

He gave them names, and drew their comrades. With pencil and watercolor he did portraits of German and American soldiers in full World War I battle dress—helmet, pack, gas mask, bayoneted rifle. They were individuals with crooked noses, red ears, cocked eyes, and jutting chins. He drew fluid, sketchy regiments advancing toward each other, dying under exploding shot and shell. And in his playroom battles, when a toy soldier died, Andrew was there, too, expiring gloriously, screaming, clutching his throat, writhing on the floor.

"As a kid," Wyeth says, "the times I liked best were when I worked out my own little life with these figures. I'm not sure I can comprehend the big world. I'm not a big powerful painter, doing great big forms. That isn't my interest."

He laid out battalions of soldiers in war games on the playroom floor—or in the "big room" where his mother left them undisturbed, frozen in their phalanxes. NC's student Peter Hurd had studied at West Point and Andrew listened raptly to little lectures on military tactics. "But," Hurd recollected, "Andy's mentality was pure romance. Not marches and countermarches and infantry confronting cavalry. It was the romance of lining up these soldiers, the visual side."

Everywhere was material for the long movie unreeling in Andrew's head. In the

As a boy, Wyeth expressed his preoccupation with brutality and death in works such as this watercolor of a World War I soldier on a battlefield.

small, cool entry room of NC's studio, shelves and cupboards were filled with World War I images. There was a stack of illustrated Sunday-newspaper sections—called the rotogravure—and a small library of stereopticon slides, which in a special viewer were three-dimensional. Andrew pored over these pictures of Germans in spike-topped helmets, of dashing air aces, of bombed towns, dead soldiers, and troops in trenches. In his mind these images of death and brutality—romantic at that distance—were like a bloodstream flowing between his paintings, his own German origins, and his toy-soldier battles.

Andrew and Ann developed a game that took the romance of war—and the hovering danger of death—so entirely into the realm of imagination that it was *totally* hidden from view. They built a railway terminal with boxes and ran model railroad tracks into the dark interior. Ann played a record called the *Victory Ball*.

She remembers, "We could just *see* the figures, their helmets, inside that ominous, dark place, and feel the confusion and terror of war, the station full of trains—the coldness, the dreariness of the curving tracks." On the Victrola record, drums rustled softly in the distance, then rattled louder and louder to a thundering, heart-pounding din of danger. "Tremendous excitement out of nothing, really," Ann says. "We did it over and over again."

Pine Baron. 1976

Wyeth's boyhood fascination with war was embodied by Karl
Kuerner, who had been a machine gunner in the German army.
Karl's wife Anna once used her husband's old helmet to gather pine
cones for kindling.

Andrew watched his war games life-sized when he was taken to the silent-movie classic *The Big Parade*—which he bought as a mature man and ran for himself hundreds of times alone in his studio, still feeding his imagination, his chidhood fantasies still fresh. On the screen, wavy lines of new recruits advanced into battle for the first time. In his mind they moved through a wood much like the one behind NC's house. Invisible in the trees were German snipers—like a German farmer-friend Karl Kuerner. Here a soldier fell, dead as straw, there another pitched forward in the terrible silence—like his toy soldiers. And still the thinning lines moved ahead, through familiar sunlit patterns of light and dark.

Everywhere there were stimulations for his dreams. He had free run of his father's huge studio up behind the house—an island of romance. From its ceiling hung a birchbark canoe. On the floor were western saddles, a tall Indian drum. Shelves lined the walls filled with source books. On top were Indian artifacts, ship models of a Spanish galleon and a two-masted schooner, plaster casts of the Marquis de Lafayette and George Washington. Three white death masks watched from one wall—near a display of World War I helmets, a canteen, and a gas mask. NC worked at paintings held on heavy wooden easels. With his broad palette like a paint-piled wing in one hand, his legs braced like an athlete's, he wielded his brush with controlled violence—and often wiped it on his ballooning knickers.

Against the walls were stacked the original paintings for NC's illustrations, the great depictions of Robin Hood meeting Maid Marian, of King Arthur in a boat receiving the sword Excalibur from the Lady of the Lake, of Blind Pew tapping his way down the moonlit road in *Treasure Island*. Andrew spent hours picking through the canvases, firing his imagination with these fierce pageants. NC willingly stopped painting to answer questions and talk about each picture. Sometimes, like the other Wyeth children, Andrew posed for a work in progress—and was paid with chocolate-covered marshmallows.

All the while, Andrew was drawing on paper his own inner pageant. That was his deepest joy, the doing of pictures, bringing his imagination to life uninhibited, showing them to nobody except sometimes NC.

When Andrew was taken to see the movie *Black Pirate,* his pencil and watercolor brush began recording the Spanish Main, drawing a vast, childish galleon bristling with pirates, two pirates dueling, another running with a cutlass in his mouth, a captain standing on his ship—with a detail by NC demonstrating the rigging.

When he was ten and eleven, medieval knights and castles were fed into his fantasy by Arthur Conan Doyle's *The White Company.* His father sometimes took him to New York and the Metropolitan Museum. While NC looked at the paintings, Andrew went to the armor exhibit, to the figures fully dressed in embossed steel—standing or astride horses under the long lines of flags.

He was thrilled by Joan of Arc's helmet with its dent from a crossbow bolt—"the most simple, beautiful object I've ever seen." He stood mesmerized by the armorer's forge with a mannequin pounding out swords and breastplates. His intensity caught the attention of a museum curator, who talked to Andrew about the exhibits and let him try on a helmet and heft the huge, two-handed swords. Wyeth still remembers the feel. "Beautifully balanced," he says with awe.

Andrew was growing up on the very ground of the battle of the Brandywine, where the British defeated Washington's troops,

Maximilian Armor. 1941
At age 24, Wyeth remained interested in the armor he studied on boyhood trips with his father to New York's Metropolitan Museum. He drew it again when the armor came on loan to the Wilmington Museum.

who then retreated to Valley Forge. He was studying the Revolutionary-period pen drawings of his father's teacher Howard Pyle, and NC entertained Andrew with drawings of the battle. When the family went to Concord, Massachusetts, Andrew was fascinated by Concord Bridge and the graves of the British soldiers killed there.

When he was twelve, the pages of his sketchbook—a Quality Bond pad of typewriter paper—seethed with the eras and epics that swirled together in his head. Peaked-hatted redcoats battled colonial troops, death everywhere. On the next page, armored knights fought, succeeded by World War I biplane fighters. Soldiers with bayonets mingled with swaggering musketeers and Robin Hood's bow-and-arrow band dressed in Lincoln green.

During those years, Andrew was just one of many Wyeth artists, all talented. *"Drawing!"* enthused NC in a letter. "That's the outstanding stunt in this house, and to see the whole five around the lamp at night, each one bent over a tablet of paper, recording all sorts of facts and fictions of Nature, one would at least guess it was organized night art school—or that all were nutty in the same way!"

When Andrew did formal pictures, illustrations imitating his revered father, the drawing was tight and awkward—careful lines filled in with watercolor. But depicting violent action, his pencil rushed down his emotion, the lines quick and confident and free. From the beginning, Andrew was a technician. Drawing a childish volcano, he was thrilled to discover that he could make the shading for the smoke by brushing the paper with the side of the lead. "It was a revelation to me," says Wyeth, excited by the memory. "If you controlled how you handled your pencil or brush, you could add something."

At thirteen, Andrew was given a special drawing pen by Peter Hurd. By fourteen, Andrew was receiving the best materials from his father. To make detailed pen drawings like those of his idol Albrecht Dürer, Andrew preferred the basic wooden pen holder with its choice of insertable points. Wyeth says, "Even when I was little, I was very sensitive to the tools I used—enjoyed the quality of that thick ink flowing out—a joy."

3
A Secret Life

Jack and Willard. 1973
Like a casualty in Wyeth's boyhood battles, his old friend Willard
Snowden lies among jack in the pulpit flowers.

Pictures were only one of the ways that Andrew animated his daydreams. Several times a week his henchmen gathered after school in the entry room of NC's studio. There a chest held the costumes that NC used when drawing his literary buccaneers and musketeers, soldiers and desperadoes, cowboys and Indians—clothing steeped in blood and thunder. His cousin Mary Sergeant remembers Andrew, his cohorts towering above his small, curly-headed figure, as he excitedly laid out the plan for the day—"incandescent with ideas."

Sometimes it was a foray for the invincible swordsman d'Artagnon and his Three Musketeers. More often it was an exploit by Robin Hood and his Merry Men—setting off through the countryside searching for adventure, "just the way Robin Hood did," Wyeth says. Andrew was clothing with action the secret charades he had lived while the others were at school. "They were doing these things just for the moment," Wyeth says. "They never knew I was doing something I'd been into all week. I never told them. To me it was sort of like building a painting."

All were steeped in the stories they were mimicking, and they dug into the chest for the costumes of the characters they usually played. Sometimes girls were included. Ann Wyeth played Robin Hood's friend Will Scarlet. Mary Sargent, who spent vacations with the Wyeths, acted Allan a Dale. Always there were a neighbor's son, Harry Armet, and Andrew's near-constant companion, a black boy named David Lawrence. He was often Friar Tuck, and Wyeth remembers, "He had great imagination; more imagination than any white boy I ever met. He dressed in black with that cowl—and his marvelous black face and the whites of his eyes. Oh, God, it was wonderful."

Andrew, the instigator, was, of course, the lead actor with first choice of outfits. As d'Artagnon, he wore a curly black wig, plumed hat, painted mustache and beard, leather vest, tall boots, and cape and carried a real rapier. As Robin Hood, he dressed in tights and a leather jerkin and a peaked cloth cap, with a real bow and quiver of arrows slung over his shoulders. The little troop fairly bristled with warlike equipment. "The more we could carry," Wyeth says, "the more we looked like the figures out of Howard Pyle and N. C. Wyeth."

Living the charade, feeling their characters inside themselves, they spoke their version of Elizabethan English, and the woods rang with cries of "Varlet!"—"Knave!"—"Fie upon thee!" Skulking through the forest, hiding from the Sheriff of Nottingham, they made secret camps, toasting each other with pretend wine in tin mugs. They baked potatoes in the coals of fires they built against the rocks—which had been drilled with holes for Revolutionary War mortars. Sometimes they changed sides and leaped out at each other from high rocks and fought not-so-mock battles with poles, called quarterstaffs, leaving each other bruised and bloody. Mary Sargent remembers Andrew and David Lawrence "having swordplay with wild gesticulations, the small white and black arms and legs making a marvelous moving design and the flashing white teeth of both displaying the savagery of the young duelists."

Once they waylayed pretty Janet Miller, daughter of the local postmistress, leaping out at her, brandishing their swords. Wyeth remembers, "Of course, I wanted to be the gallant one and save this young girl." Once they spotted a boy bringing groceries home. Taking from the rich to give to the poor, they surrounded him and grabbed the food. "Oh, my God, awful!" Wyeth says, delighted. "It wasn't all nice. We were really after blood."

By late afternoon, the fierce band would tire and drift away home. Andrew, who *was* Robin Hood, is still frustrated at the memory. "They never wanted to carry it on," he says with outrage. He adds, "I spent so much time alone, I had to build my own stories and that is the way painting has been to me—a constant new experience I want to carry through to the end."

When Errol Flynn played Robin Hood in the movie, he was exactly the swashbuckler Andrew had imagined himself, and later Wyeth purchased Flynn's pirate movies to run on NC's antique 35-millimeter projector. In 1988 Wyeth telephoned his sister Ann from Maine and said, "I'm painting Errol Flynn." He was doing an elegant, delicate, towering white yacht, designed for racing, tied up in a shipyard in

Above: **Maiden Voyage.** 1988

A toy sailboat given to Andrew for a birthday present (left) is echoed in a painting of a sloop that he watched being built at a boatyard near his Maine house. When he did this tempera, he considered painting his two hands holding the yacht.

Both N.C. and Andrew Wyeth shared a sense of the dramatic, with vivid fantasy lives that enriched their art and was expressed as well in everyday terms: here, N.C. is larger than life as he paints an illustration and shows off his new Cadillac outside the Chadds Ford house; Andrew acts a proper Musketeer.

Thomaston, Maine. A white awning shields its cockpit. Fragile gear is protected by tailored canvas covers. Behind it, blacking out the sky, looms a gargantuan pine—vast, deep with danger.

In those boyhood years, the one person who saw Andrew's work was NC—a kindly teacher, nudging Andrew in the right direction. He kept telling his son, "You must free yourself." He once redrew a musketeer's cape so that, instead of carved from stone, it was cloth flowing to the floor—and Andrew practiced it, page after page. He loved his father totally, was bound to him on every level. "Nobody ever had a greater father," Wyeth says. "I don't think a father and son could have a warmer relationship."

But this hypersensitive boy was also frightened by NC's power to overwhelm him. Andrew was a watcher. From a young age, he saw his father clearly. NC had always been a titanic figure in Andrew's life, monitoring the whole family, shaping, controlling. "He ruled 'em," remembers a young friend of Andrew's. "Part of NC's power was a streak of violence—his willingness to crush—that waited behind the kindness and poetry." Henriette once said, "Pa was the sun that moved around and you'd get burned if you got too close."

NC once described "three young squirt art students who . . . silently sniffed and sneered . . . until I flew into a rage and lashed them with my tongue within an inch of their lives. My candid attack finally cracked them into making what amounted to the most naive confessions of their tiny, insectlike, art-student point of view. You bet your bottom dollar I didn't leave them with a leg to stand on. Outside of its being a setting-up exercise for my chest and larynx, the whole hour was absurd and futile. The next bunch of bowel-running art students that approach this studio will be shot down in cold blood—for they haven't any warm blood anyway."

Peter Hurd once said, "Pa was a man of tremendous moods. Deeply, deeply complicated. He was double. If he was glowering, you braced yourself. Maybe he'd begin on some puny characteristic in my nature that he believed showed in my painting. In a few incisive words, right to the point, like a pick in a sore place, he would hit right at it. And, oh, God, you knew it was true. The next day that mood, like the clouds, would sweep away. The sun would shine. He'd build me up, point out the good things in my character and what I'd done."

These mood swings were symptoms of a central angry sorrow that overtook NC and spoiled the innocence of the wholesome, idyllic Wyeth family life. In the first seven or eight years of his marriage, NC was filled with ideals and high expectations. While producing his greatest illustrations, he talked about doing "pictures that will last, like the works of men like Michelangelo, Raphael." The year of Andrew's birth, he wrote, "Every stroke of my brush will become charged with a *cosmic* truth—the *universal message of the ages.*"

But soon after that, Henriette remembers, "Pa began to fall apart. Andy had a very different father than I did—one who was beginning to be disillusioned and sad." Andrew watched his powerful father doubt himself. NC shrugged off the illustrations Andrew loved and in later years called them "trash." When he tried to paint landscapes—reach toward great art—these pictures made no real mark. He mixed with important painters of his day, impressing them with his personality, but felt inferior—*only* an illustrator—even as he discussed his theories of art.

At this time abstract art was taking over. "My father," Andrew Wyeth remembers, "thought the art world had completely turned around." Henriette, much admired by NC, was interested in the new art, and into the house came books on Cézanne and Picasso and Braque. In easel paintings done in the studio, NC explored impressionism and abstraction. For a time he influenced his daughter Carolyn, who was also his student. Even as a boy, Andrew knew that he disagreed with his father, and in museums he left the others and searched out realist masters like Dürer, Winslow Homer, and John Constable. "Pa didn't bother much with me," Wyeth says gratefully. "I was too young."

No matter how hard NC experimented with various mediums and techniques, he did not earn the respect he craved, not even self-respect. Considering himself a failure, miserable with frustration and self-torment, he wrote his mother, "All sense of serenity has drained away, and all I can do, when I think about it, is to gawk stupidly at the retreating pageant of my dreams and hopes."

But even as his artistic self-esteem fell, NC looked for comfort in the adulation his fame and personality commanded. When he finished a painting, admirers assembled in the studio on a long bench and NC paced back and forth before them, expounding on the new work. Once a young man from the Du Pont Company in nearby Wilmington talked to the person next to him on the bench. NC, in a rage, seized him and bodily ejected him from the studio.

While watching his father's convictions wobble, Andrew also thought NC's lifestyle was a weakness, a distraction that made great painting impossible. As NC's dreams faded, he had begun enjoying his wealth—accumulated even though he was often underpaid. His output was prodigious. In his lifetime he produced 6,500 paintings, including posters, calendars, advertisements, enormous murals, illustrations for magazines and about seventy-five books. One of his finest illustrations— two train robbers battling guards between cars—he painted in a morning.

By the 1930s, NC had become something of a country squire. There was now a cook, a maid, and a butler. All laundry was sent out. NC was shaved by a barber in town. A tennis court was built. A summer house in Port Clyde, Maine, had been acquired and a huge, long dock constructed for his power boat. Enormous cars arrived in Chadds Ford, containing such celebrities as Scott and Zelda Fitzgerald. There was Joseph Hergesheimer, the flamboyant author, originally a friend of Henriette. She herself was now a dazzling young woman and social magnet in her own right. NC would sit up most of the night while Hergesheimer read manuscripts to him aloud. Other writers included Pulitzer Prize–winner Paul Horgan and Eric Knight, who did *Lassie Come Home* and *This Above All*. H. L. Mencken, the acid social critic, came up from Baltimore. Max Perkins, the celebrated Scribner's editor, was after NC to take up writing. Hollywood came to Chadds

Ford—Richard Barthelmess, Lillian Gish, John Gilbert, the star of *The Big Parade*. Douglas Fairbanks, Sr., wanted NC to move the whole family to Hollywood and direct his movie *The Black Pirate*.

At the many parties in the studio, young Andrew hung on the edges, watching and listening—and being a nuisance. When young couples went out to sit in cars, he hid underneath and made obscene mouth noises. In particular, he liked to torment Joseph Hergesheimer, who called him "that sinister demon child." Andrew would deliberately pretend to confuse him with another writer the eminent writer detested. When Hergesheimer protested, Andrew said, "Isn't that your name?" Hergesheimer bellowed, "Not by fifty years and two cross-eyes."

Andrew sneaked gulps from his siblings' drinks. One night he got tight on homemade hard cider with a boy named Skootch Talley. Hearing his father coming, Andrew jumped into bed with all his clothes on, his dog Lupe beside him. When NC came in, Andrew was blamelessly asleep—with two huge shoes sticking up from under the covers.

Andrew's sister Carolyn, however, has a mental image of the fundamental boy. He is standing apart, watching his father play tennis while distinguished guests laugh and applaud. Then Andrew, invisible as an Indian, slips away into the woods. "I was just wandering over these hills looking at things, not particularly thinking about art, just perfectly to myself," Wyeth says. "As often happens with the youngest child, my mother and father planned for the other kids, and I was just left alone without too much scrutinizing. Which delighted me." Andrew, even at that young age, had emotionally disappeared into the countryside, out from under his father. His fear of NC, and his disappointment, gradually through the years grew into a suppressed but simmering fury, triggered by anything that might threaten his work, might confine his freedom, and might start the same corruptions and interruptions he blamed for his father's decline. It became a kind of adrenaline, redoubling the intensity of his painting, a hot blood in the veins of his cool realism.

In the peace of solitude and secrecy, Andrew felt safe. Henriette remembers, "We

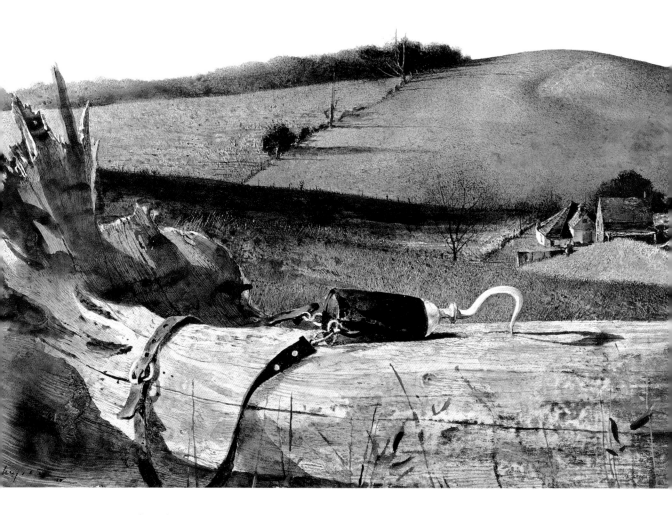

Little Africa. 1984

The title of the painting refers to N.C. Wyeth's name for the area where Andrew's black boyhood friends lived. The image also recalls Bill Loper, who wore a hook in place of his missing left hand, and in the background Mother Archie's Church.

never really knew the truth. Andy was already building an impregnable fortress made of air." All his life Wyeth has been excited by the hidden, by concealment. Each day when he leaves his home, nobody knows for sure what he will do and where. He himself refers to the "power of secrecy."

There is drama for him in the surreptitious. He and Ann worked secrets into their play. She says: "Secrecy brings an edge. Everything is enhanced. It's yours!" And hiding is a form of self-protection for Wyeth, who is a man easily angered and hurt. "I'm supersensitive," he admits. "Some little thing can ruin my whole day. But you've got to be vulnerable. Otherwise, you're no good. Keep your spirit open. That's the whole thing."

Trying to flood a picture with deep emotions, Wyeth enters a fragile self-hypnosis. In a trance of openness, he tunes into a stream of images and feelings. Like a man who can weep only in private, he dreads the judgment of others, dreads anything that might inhibit the flow. Very rarely does anybody see a painting in progress. "I might kill somebody; that's how tense I get," Wyeth says. "I don't care if it's a child making a comment. It makes me mad. Isn't that awful?"

Henriette says, "The great things are created secretly—like impregnation in the womb. The dreams in your head are secret and dark and magical and they ought to be." An example is Wyeth's series of paintings of Helga Testorf, the German wife of a Chadds Ford botanist. From 1970 to 1985 he kept them and her a secret, even from his own wife. He told a couple of friends in case anything happened to him. During those years he was repeating the spontaneity of the childhood drawings nobody saw. With Helga he was again free to do *anything,* unconcerned whether the work was good or bad. He could let the mood flow and flow, uninterrupted.

Andrew's secret ramblings became, as boy and man, a complete, secret life. The territory began at the big rocks above NC's studio and extended through a field on top of the ridge, into a wood, and across cornfields. From this high point, he looked down on the stone octagon of Mother Archie's Church and the square house of the minister, Mother Archie herself. Proceeding left, Andrew moved down a mowed hill to the farm of Karl Kuerner, a German immigrant.

His Aunt Elizabeth once described him on these walks. "Andy looked like nobody you ever knew. His body was very flexible and you knew he was seeing something only he could see—the same look when he was younger and listening to a story and he was seeing a picture in his mind's eye, just as though it was part of a landscape."

Wyeth says, "That was where I came into my own. I feel that I became an artist out of the life that I led, things that appealed to me and really excited me, and then I began to paint." Young Andrew made friends with the blacks on his route. There was Evelyn Smith, who lived next to Mother Archie's. In a log house on the ridge David Lawrence lived alone with his father, seventy-eight-year-old John Lawrence, who could jump into the air and click his heels three times before hitting the ground. There was religious Adam Johnson, a handyman who kept his house immaculate. In his fur hat and layer upon layer of clothing, he was to Andrew "like a Mongol prince, or in those jingles and safety pins, Old Chris."

By age fourteen, in addition to soldiers and knights, Wyeth was painting primitive watercolors of these people and places on his walk. There was Bill Loper, fascinating with a hook for a left hand. Drawing him cutting wood next to Mother Archie's house, Andrew concealed the hook behind Loper's body. NC, who thought his son was wasting his time with such people, had told Andrew the hook was too shocking to be shown.

These blacks let this white boy from over the hill into their lives—an intimacy Wyeth has always been able to earn. In the semi-outcasts, the misunderstoods, he finds the quality nobody else has seen, the inner dignity, the hidden virtue that makes them special and valuable, makes them a medium for Wyeth's imagination.

Traveling this small world, feeling the timelessness of the rocks and hills, reflecting on the people who had come and gone there—became throughout Wyeth's life central to his work. One fall afternoon in later years, walking through the rows of corn, Wyeth imagined how a king must have felt moving down a line of knights on horseback with banners blowing. "I can think of nothing more exciting," he once said, "than just sitting in the corn on a windy day and listening to the dry rustle. I love to study the many things that grow below the cornstalks. If one

could catch that true color of nature! The very thought of it drives one mad."

Wyeth rose at three o'clock one moonlit night and walked in ecstasy through fields where a small, wet snowstorm had coated each twig and blade of grass. In the dusk of dawn, windows clicked on one by one with lights—his black friends stirring. By then they included tall, stately, blue-eyed Tom Clark, who lived alone by the railroad tracks with his retarded son. For years Andrew dropped in on them, watching rapt as Tom's spidery hand ceremoniously raised the lid of a boiling pot of cabbage, as though a wonderful gift lay inside. Every chore was an all-important art—the potato peel coiling off Tom's knife in a continuous ribbon. Eventually,

Opposite: **Black Hunter.** 1939

Still experimenting with his new medium, tempera, Wyeth portrayed David Lawrence, his familiar companion in many early dress-up escapades.

Right: Andrew poses for a snapshot with his friend Ben Loper, whose house was a regular stop in his visits to Little Africa.

Wyeth painted Tom's long figure on the patchwork quilt of his garret bed—a picture based in part on a boyhood Christmas Eve.

Wyeth, remembering, says "I woke up in a sweat and reached out in the dark and felt for the bottom of the stocking my father had hung on the end of the bed. I crept with my fingers up it and felt the different shapes. There was this strange figure made out of wood with big feet and a marvelous head with a pointed hat. I wondered what it was; I couldn't put the light on because my father would raise hell if we woke up too soon. I remember clutching it to me and smelling the new paint on its face and feeling the nose and wondering. When I painted old Tom Clark lying on a quilt on his bed, people often said how long his body was—that thin figure with that pointed nose and rather big feet. It all came from that night before Christmas."

One evening, fourteen-year-old Andrew had been drawing the sheep at a farm owned by an old bachelor, known as Spud Murphy because he lived on bread and potatoes. Wyeth remembers, "In the dusk he turned and walked in back of his pigpens into a grove of apple trees. He had on a square beaver hat and a sheepskin coat, and he turned a little, and I remember seeing his back, and the light on his face. And I remember I became terribly excited."

In that instant, that conjunction of figure and light and mood, Andrew's fantasy and real life collided for the first time in a single, horrific jolt. He felt in his soul that this might be Mr. Hyde on his way home. Or Dracula was there behind a pigpen, glimpsed like a lightning flash in a black room. Andrew knew now that to find horror, the most electrifying of all excitements; he did not have to go to books. Halloween was alive in the landscape waiting to be painted.

"It was a very queer thing and it began everything," Wyeth says. "I wanted to explain it to Pa, and didn't know how to do it." NC, the presiding officer of Andrew's life, who had told him in a flat New England voice that these walks were a waste of time, could not be trusted to understand. He might shrivel the thrilling connection Andrew himself only half understood. More than ever, Andrew went underground. He did not want his father to know his true feelings about what he drew, did not want *anybody* to know.

"That's why I like to be free," Wyeth explains about his walks. "Real emotions happen so rarely they are hard to come by. Not synthetic emotion, but emotion that tears your insides out. You want to be ready for it." Wyeth continues, "Sometimes I don't even know I'm walking, don't even know I'm there. I like to be nothing. I wish I could float over all this. And that's, of course, the effect I'm after in my painting."

If he is too conscious of himself, Wyeth believes, he may miss that thrilling flash that inspires a painting, that image seen "out of the corner of the eye, off balance," that intersection of light and movement and imagination. The sun on the side of a

Wyeth was photographed in 1965 as he painted Ralph Cline for a tempera called **The Patriot.** The artist had first seen Cline marching at the head of a Memorial Day parade in Maine, wearing an old army veteran's uniform. Cline agreed to have his portrait painted, and the many long sittings took place in a room above the sawmill owned by Cline. After the posing was finished, Cline said, "One thing Andy's got is unlimited patience. He'd work all day on something and he'd come back the next morning and if it didn't suit him, he rubbed it right out."

hill or a rim of light on the curve of an arm can start a rush of memories, of feelings, of horror—like Spud Murphy, like Dracula behind the pigpen.

Sometimes such moments do not emerge in a painting for years, held in Wyeth's memory bank, combining with other images and their emotions, other pieces of the vast mosaic. But most often, as he says, "My hair rises on the back of my head. And I can't think of going anywhere or doing anything but grab that thing."

He makes a feverish sketch on a handy piece of paper, trying to fix what it was that excited his imagination. His brush may spread only a simple tone, his pencil scribble the roughest image. A painting called *Lime Banks* was for weeks a single pregnant line, the top of the bank drawn across the white wall of his tiny studio in Maine. "I may look at a sketch for months," Wyeth says. "It keeps my mind working. I dream a lot. I do more painting when I'm not painting."

"Dreaming" is Wyeth's word for his amazing stream of consciousness, mingling present and past, truth and fantasy, natural and supernatural—seamless, simultaneous, forever secret. It is Wyeth's way of seeing. It lies at the center of his art. Only occasionally, when he speaks about a picture, does Wyeth give hints of what is under the surface.

In Maine he painted seventy-one-year-old Ralph Cline wearing a World War I uniform. Afterward, Wyeth talked about the rotogravure sections in his father's studio. "I can remember the smell of that newspaper, the pictures, the page of the casualty list, pictures of General Pershing, Frank Luke the Balloon Buster, or Rickenbacker or Captain Whittlesey of the Lost Battalion, or even the tunic of the man who was killed in Serbia at the start of the war. That could be the tunic Ralph has on. All that faded into the picture I wanted to paint—my truth behind the fact. I kept thinking about his bald head, that round oval, while I was driving in my car, lying in bed—the bald light top where his hat always was, which could be the head of the American bald eagle. In that curve along the top of the head was the essence of what excited me. It was the whole beginning of the painting."

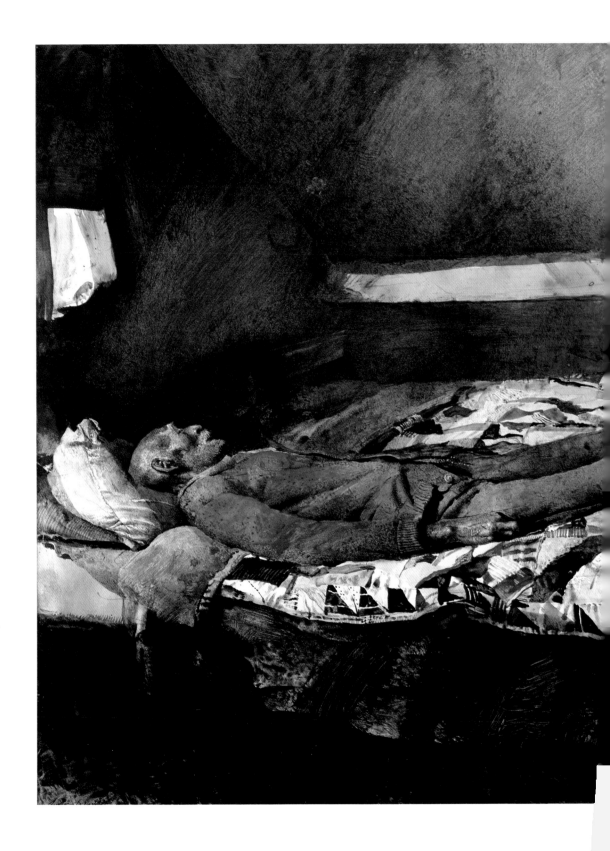

Soaring. 1950

The turkey vulture's view of the hills of Wyeth's little patch of Pennsylvania dramatizes the atmosphere of many of the artist's paintings—a feeling that a spirit has returned to the world and hovers, studying people, their relationships, and objects that reflect their daily lives.

Adam. 1963
Pencil study for **Adam.** 1963

Preparing to paint the large tempera of Adam Johnson, Wyeth, as he does with all major works, made pencil or watercolor sketches to master the "feel" and structure of details, such as Adam's fur hat and collar. He did much the same in pencil sketches of a vulture's wingspread for **Soaring**. These "notes" are mere facts to guide his hand. His final painting reshapes and simplifies reality, creating not a replica but his private vision, including his memory of the subject, his feelings about it, and the quality that first triggered his imagination.

Garret Room. 1962

Tom Clark was always at home for Wyeth, allowing Andrew into the orderly and intimate routines of his life. Wyeth's dream has always been to become so submerged in the life of his subjects that he would be virtually invisible. He could thus achieve an intimacy that would saturate the paintings.

4
Into the World Alone

Wind from the Sea. 1947

Though she is not physically present here, this painting is a kind of portrait of Christina Olson. He was stimulated to think of it by opening a window in a stiflingly hot room of her house and a fresh wind billowed the curtains. To Wyeth, the delicacy of the embroidered birds echoed Christina's refined spirit that survived the wear and tear of time.

In 1932, when Andrew was fifteen, NC saw one of his son's plays and it convinced him that the boy's fantasy life—that boiling imagination—should now be harnessed by fundamental academic training. This particular play was "Robin Hood," presented in a tiny white and gold theater with a red muslin stage curtain and two tiers of little box seats on each side. It sat on a tabletop, and blankets, hung from a rope, surrounded its proscenium arch. The family was solemnly gathered. In their hands were penciled programs listing the scenes: "Robin's Home—Archery at Nottingham—In Sherwood Forest—The Blue Boare Inn—Death of Robin Hood."

While Ann played the music on the phonograph, painted cardboard bowmen and swordsmen, pikemen in helmets, Robin's Merry Men in jerkins and cloth hats, Robin himself, blond and handsome, moved across the stage, towed by strings. Behind them were elaborately painted sets—an inn room with wood rafters, a grandstand filled with Elizabethan ladies and courtiers. Andrew did all the voices:

"My Lady, don't you think it is nigh time for Robin to go out in search of adventure?"

"Why, yes, my Lord."

"Robin! Robin!"

"I shall come at once, my Lord."

"Robin, I think you should go into the world alone in search of adventure. A week from today you will go."

After drawing his last childhood fantasy picture—a huge and remarkable pen and ink panorama of a medieval army laying siege to a castle—Andrew entered his father's studio with the other students. For several months he drew cubes and cones and spheres against white paper—and learned his father's intense respect, almost a reverence, for the subjects of a painting, no matter how simple. Henriette, remembering her own lessons, says, "Pa would describe the shadows that shaped the sphere, the dark underneath, like a black feather, then a smoky dusk, and then the reflected light with its kind of starlit double edge. He would say, 'That light proceeds from the sun that has shone on the Roman emperors and Jesus himself—and here it falls on this sphere.'"

Next NC promoted Andrew to careful drawings of still lifes and plaster casts. When Andrew was seventeen, NC introduced him to oil painting. By eighteen, he was doing impressive paintings of bottles and drapery and portraits of friends—George Kipe, one of Robin Hood's Merry Men, and David Lawrence. Andrew disliked oil, its smell and greasiness, and the stubbiness of the brushes, but he dared not defy his father.

NC never taught technique. He did not believe there were set ways to apply paint, formulas for composition or prescriptions for laying in a sky or drawing hair. "How to paint a picture," Wyeth says, "is something I worked out alone by trial and error." NC did teach a basic principle of Andrew Wyeth's art: the certainty that if emotions for the object are strong enough and focused enough, they will bypass the brain, travel down the arm, and in some magic way, flow onto the blank surface.

NC himself, after a morning at work on a grimacing character, would come down from the studio with his own face aching from baring his teeth. Peter Hurd has said, "Pa taught us to equate ourselves with the object, become the very object itself. Andy does that. He makes people of things, and that person is also himself, and vice versa. It's a curious, wonderful thing."

While Andrew was studying with his father and dreaming in the countryside, he was receiving another kind of education from Peter Hurd, an experienced lady's man who in time became Henriette's fiancé and a surrogate brother-father to Andrew. Janet Miller remembers Hurd's arrival at age twenty in his western boots and Stetson hat. "He was a swashbuckling man if there ever was one," she says. "When he hit Chadds Ford, we all stood up and looked."

Hurd thought Andrew was getting "the genius treatment" in the family, and was too protected by NC, who had a New England prudish streak and once told

Henriette she must never pose a woman with legs apart. Hurd educated Andrew in matters of sex—encouraging him in an affair with an older girl. "Pa would have killed him," Wyeth says, "if he had known what Pete was telling me."

Hurd imposed on Andrew some of the rigor absorbed during the two years at West Point. Wyeth says, "He was tough on me; taught me fencing." In 1929 Hurd married Henriette. NC insisted that they remain in Chadds Ford, and for a decade they contented themselves with periodic trips to New Mexico—before finally moving to their ranch in San Patricio, where Billy the Kid lived as a boy. During one of Hurd's absences, Andrew took fencing lessons from the captain of the University of Pennsylvania team. Wyeth remembers with satisfaction, "Pete came back and said, 'Let's fence.' Well, he was shocked. I fenced him right off the porch."

It was Henriette who taught Andrew to dance and how to dress, so he could join his siblings at parties in Wilmington society, centered around the du Pont family.

Above: **Lobster Traps.** 1939
This is an example of the colorful, flamboyant watercolors that
Andrew painted until the death of his father.

Opposite, above: When the 20-year-old artist Peter Hurd came to
study with N.C. Wyeth he became a friend and mentor for young
Andrew. Here they are seen at Rehoboth Beach, Delaware. A few
years later Hurd introduced Andrew to painting in the medium of
tempera, a combination of egg yolks and powdered pigment.

Janet Miller became his first girlfriend. Henriette says, "From sixteen on, Andy
was a Beau Brummel, very handsome, looked just marvelous with this sort of
conscious actor's expression. Smooth as cream. Suave. A great lover and all that.
John Barrymore stuff."

Fundamentally, however, Andrew remained a loner. The closest he came to an intimate friend was a piratical Maine fisherman named Walt Anderson, a Swedish-Finnish boy with some Indian blood, who seemed to Andrew a Viking reborn. Andrew, now the owner of a driver's license, could escape each spring to Maine months ahead of his father and family. In a seacoast version of his Pennsylvania ramblings, Andrew and Walt spent most of their days afloat in a dory, shooting the surf that broke over reefs and hauling lobstermen's pots at night to swipe the dinner they cooked on the island where they camped. Once they stole two dozen ears of corn from a seaside patch while the owner was hoeing the opposite end. NC never approved of that friendship. Andrew's father considered Walt beneath his son—and not a fit subject for pictures.

Painting Walt, painting the white wood houses clinging to rock ledges, the deep surge of the ocean, and the diamond clarity of light—Andrew was becoming a master of watercolor. The pigment soaked out into the white paper from the wet camel's-hair brushes—a sky, a sea washed in by a few strokes, the details of a boat, a bird done in quick, sure stabs. It was the natural medium for the wild and messy side of Andrew's nature. Peter Hurd has described Wyeth "slashing at the work as if with a stiletto, dabbing with a bit of Kleenex, and slashing with a razor blade. He looks like he's in battle." Wyeth explains, "You come on something in nature and you're excited. Maybe the weather is stormy and you have terrific feelings. If you can get them down before you begin to think, they you get something."

To Andrew, these pictures contained "the smell and taste of the color of Maine . . . the encrustation and the barnacled rocks and sun and shadowy days and the feeling of sea and salt air." He says, "They had a kind of joyous excitement.

Adrift. 1982
Wyeth painted his old friend Walt Anderson lying down in a boat and looking something like a body floating out to sea in a Viking funeral. At left, a pencil sketch of the dory.

They were a portrait of how I felt at the time. You paint what you are. I was soaking up the country, and I wasn't ready to express anything." NC admired those paintings. "He was really excited by my watercolors," Wyeth says. "He felt *my* excitement."

But NC did not think his son could make a living as a watercolorist. Though he himself had compromised his own dreams in order to make a living, NC was grooming his son to be an illustrator. Andrew did pen and ink illustrations that were published under NC's name. Under his own name, Andrew did a picture for a new edition of the works of Howard Pyle. He illustrated Conan Doyle's *Sir Nigel*, which his father unsuccessfully tried to sell.

When Andrew graduated from his father's studio at seventeen, NC faced the fact that his son was the artist he himself could never be. Andrew had taken an illustration job from the publisher Little, Brown & Co. and postponed his usual early-spring move to Maine. But the more he read the manuscript the worse it seemed. "It was *awful!*" Wyeth remembers. "But I struggled with it. I went to bed and was fretfully sleeping because of this goddamned book I had to do—and early in the morning this big figure stood over the bed." NC told him, "Andy, it's utterly ridiculous for you to do that book. Go to Maine and paint like hell! I will support you." Then NC released him. "You don't have to be an illustrator."

In 1937, at the age of twenty, Andrew had his first one-man show at the William Macbeth Gallery in New York City. After seeing the assembled watercolors before they were shipped, NC wrote to his son in Maine, "They are *magnificent,* and with no reservations whatsoever, they represent the *very best* watercolors I ever saw! This remark from your old dad may not mean much to you, but . . . I'm certain I'm right. You are headed in a direction that should finally reach a pinnacle in American art and so establish a landmark for all time."

All twenty-three paintings were sold before the end of the second day. Several were bought by museums. NC wrote about the work: "What magic power that boy has. I am at once stimulated beyond words to new, purer effort, and plunged into black despair." Then came the inevitable day when a young watercolorist said to NC, "By God, are you the father of Andrew Wyeth?" Telling this in a letter, NC added disgustedly, "I had trouble shaking loose from him."

Throughout these years, Andrew had relished his quick success with flashy watercolors. But he began to feel a shallowness in them, to feel that the drawing was "flimsy," without enough reality. "I got depressed," he remembers, "because the object looked like a painted thing. I felt it was so great, why lose it in paint?" And Wyeth says today, "I feel the object is the art, not what I make of it."

Andrew had already begun experimenting with a new painting medium. Peter Hurd, who had made NC into *his* father figure, was quietly rebelling in his own painting. He returned from a trip out West with a new technique called tempera. An antique medium used by the Renaissance masters, tempera is dry pigment mixed with egg yolk and distilled water and applied to a plaster-coated panel. Drying almost immediately, it requires tremendous speed and accuracy, but can achieve the most delicate detail and delivers a smooth, arid, translucent surface with no shine. At first Andrew tried to brush the pigment out like watercolor. By the time he was twenty, after two years of struggle and studying with Hurd the early examples on display at the Philadelphia Museum, he began to believe tempera could be the best medium to express his emotions.

On his twenty-second birthday, taking his first day off from painting in four months, Andrew drove away from his father's house in Maine, with its uniformed maid, houseguests, and silver brought up from Chadds Ford. The day before, he had met Merle James, a newspaper editor and competent amateur painter who had come calling on NC. Interested by James, a man filled with information, Andrew accepted his invitation to come see "our side" of the river. Circling the end of the St. George River, Andrew arrived in the town of Cushing.

Until then, Andrew's Maine experience had been the water and Walt Anderson. He had a powerful first impression of the James farm—"the wonderful rural feeling, blowing grasses, a strange open quality. I think a lot of it went into *Christina's World*." He parked and knocked on the door.

Andrew was by now wholly formed. Tallish, slender, with close-cropped, blond, hair, he radiated an exhilarating excitement, the man still filled with the impish boy. Laughter took him over completely. "Andy was the sprite of the family," Henriette says. "Always was, and still is." His square, handsome face was remarkably expressive—a rubber face capable of hysterical and horrifying distortions. Able to imitate any accent, his voice was hypnotic and poetic, as rich with moods as his paintings. When he grew excited, it became high like his father's. If he had not been a painter, Wyeth might have been a major actor.

The farmhouse door was opened, he remembers, "by this brown girl with this black hair. She was in shorts and *very* attractive." Her name was Betsy. She was

Detail of **Distant Thunder.** 1961
Finding his wife Betsy asleep under her hat while she was out berry picking, Wyeth was moved to paint an affectionate portrait.

Detail of **Maga's Daughter.** 1966
Betsy Wyeth's resemblance to her mother, whom Andrew loved very much, triggered a portrait with an antique riding hat.

66

seventeen and about to start her freshman year at Colby Junior College in New London, New Hampshire. She was Andrew's future wife.

She came from East Aurora, New York, where her father was the editor of the rotogravure section of the *Courier Express* in Buffalo. Betsy's mother, Elizabeth, nicknamed Maga, was a tall, serious woman with a strong personality, who was cursed with frail health. She had a weak heart from childhood rheumatic fever.

"Andy and I both grew up as solitary, out-of-the-mainstream children with a powerful parent," Betsy says. "I was the youngest. He was the youngest. They left me alone. They left him alone. He was a slow developer. I was very slow, the plodder, with lots of books going home at night and being sure my homework was done and very conscientious." Her sister Gwen, only fourteen months older, was intellectually quick and involved early with boys, with wearing cosmetics and painting her fingernails. Betsy was uninterested, as she puts it, "in those things that girls are supposed to do—like sports." Until fourteen, her figure a stick, she was shy and introverted.

At age fifteen Betsy discovered her powers. Suddenly she was vivacious, with flashing black eyes, exuberant, wild—and beautiful. Her sister Gwen remembers, "My God, she took off. Had all the boys around her. I thought, 'My goodness, my little sister has grown up—without my permission.'"

But Betsy's sensitivity and independence—and her secret life—remained. After the dutiful hours required at school, she stole away on her private adventures, exploring the lives of friends, age eighty and down. Like Andrew, Betsy had always been a watcher, a girl apart, who studied the undercurrents around her. "I was always fascinated with contrast," she says, "things appearing to be other than what they really were."

Betsy wanted to understand and know and be a listener for people in the odd corners of life, but not tied down. She wanted to experience their existence, wanted, as she puts it, "to smell, touch, and feel and then walk away. I wanted my freedom and I wanted to be able to move any way I wanted to go, not to be held in."

Andrew Wyeth was instantly different from all other people. Betsy remembers, "We talked about the country, talked about the quality of the light on the floor, talked about the buildings—not about college and the things that bored me stiff. I couldn't wait to get him in the car and go to Olsons'. Much more important than introducing him to my family."

A few miles down the road, set high above the St. George River, was the looming, three-story house of Christina and Alvaro Olson, brother and sister. In the days of Christina's sea-captain grandfather, Samuel Hathorn, it had been a spanking white. Now the parched clapboards were weathered silver gray from decades of wind and sun. Andrew sat on top of his car and did a watercolor of the house.

Christina had been for years a sort of summertime maiden aunt for Betsy. "Olsons' was a place I could go and be understood and adored and given total freedom," she says. "I came from a rather intellectual home, and I was fascinated by the contrast between our life and that life."

The daughter of a Swedish seaman, Christina had grown up in the house and stayed on with Alvaro to take care of her parents until their death. She had been an intensely feminine young woman with a lame leg, tall, her long hair braided or wound on top of her head. Often she wore pink dresses and white shoes. Known for her fine cooking and delicate needlework, she was house proud, keeping her home immaculate. New kittens slept in a basket padded with a damask napkin. Field flowers filled vases—and lay embroidered on her pillowcases. When Andrew met

Weather Side. 1965

Seeking to record what he loves before it is swept away, Wyeth often paints precise portraits. Here, he pictures the dried-out clapboard skin of the Olson house in Maine stretched over its cracking bones. The bucket of well water represents Alvaro Olson, who always refused to pose for Wyeth.

her, all this was still within her. "She's just like blueberries to me," Wyeth once said.

When he first arrived at Olsons', time and forced neglect had been doing its work. Christina's lameness was undiagnosed polio, and her legs had gradually weakened until, unable to walk, she spent most of her days in a kitchen chair, its legs worn off short from being pushed across the floor to the stove. To get to another room, she lowered her body to the floor and pulled herself with her arms. In her stoic pride and independence, she always refused help—even crutches or a wheelchair. And Alvaro had quietly stopped the life he loved, lobstering on the sea, in order to work the farm and care for his sister as best he could.

Alvaro, overwhelmed, exhausted, plowed up his fields of vegetables and planted blueberries, reducing his farming to a few chores—tending the geraniums in the window and the stove's wood box. All else—the land, the barn, the house, and everything in them—sat undisturbed where it had been left, turned over to the natural processes of decay. In one room stood an ancient Christmas tree, tinder-dry, its needles a brown shadow beneath it, its limbs and twigs bare as claws. The grime around the kitchen wall was lighter at the bottom, a memorial to the last day Christina could crawl there to scrub with a rag.

In the years that followed, Wyeth returned again and again to Olsons'. Christina posed for many pictures; Alvaro for only one. Allowed the run of the house, Wyeth painted objects that embodied them both—like the seed corn Alvaro had hung up to dry years earlier in a garret room. One day in a stifling bedroom, Wyeth opened a window that had been shut for years. A salt breeze, like the breath of long-dead ships and sailors, lifted the ragged lace curtains embroidered with small birds— images of Christina's delicacy of spirit.

But the spectacular decay was not what excited Wyeth. It was the decades and decades of accumulated past alive in that place. It was Alvaro's stories of an ancestor swept from a yardarm in a storm at sea. It was the sailors who had taken bearings on that edifice gleaming on its hill. It was Christina remembering the last four-master that passed down the river, watching through a spyglass the ships going out to sea, reading of storms, and waiting for their return—as she had waited for her father's ship. "There was a haunting feeling," Wyeth says, "of people coming back to a place, and ghosts of lost sailors—as though it was the tombstone of the men lost at sea."

But what brought Wyeth back and back was his friendship—really love—for Christina, a person whose great value was hidden away. Beholden to no one, supremely dignified no matter her condition, she was an unsentimental survivor, conquering pain and humiliation with self-sufficient strength and calm. To Wyeth she was everything finest about Maine. He once said, "When you get next to something as mammoth as she is, the grime and slight things evaporate and you see before you the queen of Sweden sitting there, looking at you. Small minds pick up a speck of dirt on her leg and are clouded by that. She's fabulous for me. Puts me right back on my knees."

The day after Betsy took Andrew to Olsons', he returned by boat to invite her around to Port Clyde to meet his father. Betsy insisted on bringing her sister Gwen. A week later Andrew took Betsy dancing in Rockland—and proposed to her. She accepted. "I knew at some point," she says, "somebody was going to find me and know what I was all about. And it happened. Just like that. Boom!"

NC begged Andrew not to get married. It would, he argued, interfere with Andrew's painting. Forced to support a family, he would not be able to paint the way he wanted. Wyeth remembers, "My father tried to bribe me." If he would stay single, NC promised to build him a studio at Chadds Ford and carry him financially. But the engagement was announced, and NC wrote to Henriette, "Her family are, or at least seem to be, solid, sensible people. As long as such an event must happen, it is deeply gratifying not to have to worry about what is a girl's background."

That fall Betsy entered Colby Junior College, but dropped out to get married on May 15, 1940. At the end of the ceremony, Andrew fell into his father's arms and they both wept.

5
The Crossing

Betsy and Andrew Wyeth are seen here in **Her Room** (pages 10-11),
in the house where they spend the summers in Maine by the St.
George River below her parents' farm.

Andrew and Betsy honeymooned alone in the Wyeth house in Port Clyde. When Betsy suggested they take a trip, Andrew said no. He wanted to get back to painting. He'd taken off five full days. In Chadds Ford they moved into the old schoolhouse at the foot of the road. NC had bought it for Henriette and Peter Hurd. But now Henriette had finally agreed to settle permanently in New Mexico. When Betsy took over, there were only a stove and a refrigerator. Among the first things moved in were wooden boxes filled with toy soldiers, which were soon set up on the living room bookshelves.

Betsy and NC did not get along. Betsy remembers, "It was very, very uncomfortable to be alone with him. He didn't know what to talk to me about. He thought I was shallow—that I really didn't deserve his son. I thought he was a horse's ass." Years later, she edited a collection of his letters. "When I got into them, I was *really* amazed," she says. "It wasn't till then that I saw his real quality."

Andrew and Betsy constantly had dinner up at the N. C. Wyeths' house, and every morning NC stopped by the schoolhouse to deliver their mail and talk with his son. Only occasionally now did Andrew drop by his father's studio, but still NC would come down from the studio and tell Carolyn Wyeth, "I've just had the most marvelous talk with Andy. If only I was ten years younger!"

But while trying to buck up his father, Andrew felt secretly disloyal. He believed NC did not really understand him, and he still feared his father's power to derail his work. Unable to take a stand against NC, Andrew hid pictures and kept his emotional and painting life underground.

He made Betsy his accomplice, part of the secret. In the close quarters of the schoolhouse, she was allowed into his working process, and they talked long about his work and ideas and beliefs—"These strange feelings," Betsy says, "that we'd had together, the possibility of what people could be underneath." All of that was kept from NC.

Betsy understood and believed in Andrew's goals—and very early became the lioness at the gates. She freed him in every way she could. She took over such practical matters as the family finances, such as they were. As Ann says, "They were living on two cents." She ended the teacher-student relationship between Andrew and NC.

Andrew had been doing an Indian's head for a book jacket. Betsy walked into the studio and found her new husband standing to one side while his father, brush in hand, worked on the Indian's face. Stalking out, she slammed the door like thunder. NC never again touched his son's work.

Betsy had no art training and never took any interest in her own father's painting. But she, like Andrew, was a watcher who dealt in essences, and shared his solitary fascinations. She had her own knowledge of terror beneath placid surfaces. As a girl, her bedroom was in sight of the window of a neighbor girl who was tormented by epilepsy. On quiet nights, horrifying screams curdled the darkness. So Betsy tuned in to the Halloween in Andrew's nature, the dark side that gives certain paintings their eerie strangeness, the touch of horror. She says, "He really had so much to give us in this strange world he believed in and let me see—and shared mine, too."

By nature she disliked sentimentality—what she called "softness" and "slick-ness." Instinctively she knew that her husband's unique vision, his chaos of passion, should be on the flat surface of his paintings. She asked simple questions about his watercolors, questions with the power of innocence. She wanted to know, "Why do you see so many colors. *I* don't see them. Why is that sky lavender when I see it's blue? Why aren't you painting Walt Anderson as he really is?"

Betsy says ruefully, "I guess he quickly learned that I was a girl who wasn't very artistic." But her own memory and imagination were strongly visual. From the beginning, she had a clarity that saw what was crucial—especially as Andrew gradually taught her his own way of seeing, and as it became a kind of language between them. When Andrew flashed a first sketch, she knew what had excited him. Her enthusiasm was intoxicating. But she was also a voice of truth—usually one sentence dropped into a still pool of self-satisfaction. "Betsy gets to the core of the thing,"

Wyeth says. "Maybe before we go to bed, she makes one remark. A hint is all an artist needs." Not long after their marriage, Andrew had a local show. Afterward Betsy said to him, "You paint like a very fine, well-raised, well-trained young man. I just wish you could break through to the end, get more *involved*." Wyeth remembers, "That was all I needed. Anybody gives me that lead, I always overdo it."

In the next few years, she kept urging him to paint his poignancy and anger, his sensitivity to the brutality of men and life, and the strange fantasy world he inhabited. But she also urged him to suppress the feelings, to cover them over with realism and "make the whole painting a metaphor." She told him, "Don't show all your cards, not every blade of grass. I'm not impressed."

She supported Andrew's increasing concentration on tempera, though the medium did not seem commercial. He was attracted by its finicky difficulty. He loved building tones on tones, layers of tans and rich blacks and browns and golds. He liked the natural colors from the earth, the dried, golden texture—"like a wasp's nest." Wyeth says, "It was something I could chew on for months at a time and pour myself into, create a whole world all my own." He continues, "I'm not interested in rich, warm colors. I wanted something that expresses the country." Oil paint's heavy buildup seemed to him "wet and slimy." he says, "I'm an excitable person, sure. But I'm a dry person, really. I'm not a juicy painter. There's no fight in oils. It doesn't have the austere in it, that strange removed quality, almost like a ghost."

Tempera was another break with NC, who tried it himself without understanding the medium. Andrew's subject matter, the moody, monochrome simplicity of these paintings, mystified NC. "My father gave me hell," Wyeth says. "He thought I was going down the wrong road. He said, 'You won't sell any of those pictures.'"

Overleaf: **Cornflowers.** 1986
Wyeth painted at Karl Kuerner's farm for more than 50 years. This recent watercolor shows Karl's 87-year-old wife Anna, a compulsive worker, raking field grass.

Ground Hog Day. 1959
On the ground outside the Kuerner's kitchen, a jagged-edged log
reminded Wyeth of the family's German shepherd.

In 1942 Andrew painted *Turkey Pond,* showing Walt Anderson from behind,
walking through waist-high, amber salt grass. NC said it was too empty. He
suggested adding a dog and giving Walt a rifle. That would make it more commercial, NC said.

When Betsy first came to Chadds Ford, she was lonely. Nicholas was not yet born and she felt out-of-place in the Wyeth family. Much as she had discovered Christina and Alvaro Olson, she wandered by herself to Karl Kuerner's farm and made friends with his two older daughters, who as Germans were regarded with suspicion by the town. Betsy sewed clothes with them, piled into their car and went to farm sales, tobogganed down the back hill.

At home, in their shared language of undercurrents, she and Andrew talked about Kuerners', about Mrs. Kuerner who had not wholly survived the family's traumatic move from Germany. Anna Kuerner's mind had receded into itself, a retreat into silence, broken occasionally by murmuring in German—while her tiny body darted through the farm, dawn to late night, on a compulsive round of chores. As she passed, Betsy would take her hand.

Karl Kuerner was a stumpy, softly accented man who ruled his household with iron authority. He had grown up in Germany's Black Forest. He was a machine gunner in World War I and told Andrew that he had lowered the muzzle of his gun and sprayed the fallen bodies just to make sure. He had stories about the battles at Verdun. He still had his uniform and helmet—and a picture of himself receiving a medal from the German crown prince. Karl was wounded in his right hand and arm, and on cold days had no feeling in his fingers. He would think he had pulled a knife from his pocket, only to find his hand empty.

Karl left Germany in 1923 because of the postwar inflation, spending all his money on the ship's passage. In a Philadelphia slaughterhouse he earned enough to buy the farm—which always seemed to Wyeth like the one set up under the Christmas tree for his sister Carolyn or like the farms that he and Ann built in the dirt with toy animals and tractors.

The Kuerner farm became one touchstone of his life, his father's house the other. This transplanted corner of Germany contained virtually all the boyhood fantasy that he was now beginning to paint, the themes that would grow increasingly intense through the decades. There was Wyeth's fascination with everything

German, with war, with the capacity for brutality, with impending violence. There was even in his imagination Switzerland and Christmas and Robin Hood.

In his little valley, Kuerner practiced the fundamental brutality of ground-level survival, the self-sufficiency Wyeth has always admired—everything done oneself, nothing wasted. When a groundhog was shot, it was boiled up for the dog. When a cow was too narrow to give birth, Karl saved the mother by reaching inside her with a knife and cutting out the dead calf, piece by piece. Stately trees were ruthlessly cut down at the slightest sign of decay. The farm would reverberate with the cracks of a high-powered rifle, as Karl hunted in the woods and fields—perhaps shooting a deer, which he hung up by the hind feet, blood pouring from the nose onto the snow. Even that whiteness could not completely cloak the raw brutality. But, like NC, Karl had a poetic side. In the spring he would show Andrew the first snowdrops blooming by the springhouse.

Roaming unimpeded, Andrew took the pulse of the Kuerners' house and read its deeper moods and meanings. He watched its life through the windows, felt the life in the rooms around him, guessed it from the clues he found. Burnt matches beside a lamp set him to imagining that midnight errand.

More than any other theme, Wyeth has painted the hints of the horrible that he sees among the pure. At Kuerners', the back entryway was cool and fresh as Alpine air—but on pegs hung rifles and binoculars, like the equipment of the snipers in *The Big Parade*. Wood smoke from the cooking stove scented the house and cured the hams high inside the chimney, the meat from pigs Karl slaughtered and hung in the springhouse. The sun moved across the delicately flowered wallpaper—and also across the ferocious German shepherd sleeping on the floor. In the low-ceilinged attic rooms, the plaster walls were white as a nunnery. But from those ceilings arced sinister hooks, dating back to the Revolution, used for hanging sausage. The impressionable young Andrew was told that under the hooks a hired hand had once raped a black woman.

Andrew loved the feel of those rooms, the windows deeply recessed in the stone walls as in a castle keep. He could hear from outside the sound of water overflowing the small pond—and knew that in the barn it flowed, too, out of a stone watering trough that seemed like a medieval coffin. Daily in the attic rooms wailed the whistle of the train at the crossing a hundred yards down the road—like the bellowing call of his father.

Through the house moved the tiny figure of Anna Kuerner—an iron spirit in a cloth kerchief. She was joined in Wyeth's imagination years later by Helga Testorf, who had also emigrated from Germany. She, too, had been marked by war. Her father had fought for the Nazis in World War II and she had been strafed by Russian planes. She lived across the road from the Kuerners and came to clean and care for Karl, who now in 1970 was ill with cancer. Soon Wyeth began painting her, as she became part of his associations at Kuerners'.

In those first years of marriage, in the early 1940s, Andrew had exactly the life he wanted. He had a beautiful wife who completely believed in and backed him. He was perfecting his command of tempera, which promised to be a medium for major paintings. He was surrounded by the family cocoon of his childhood, almost intact. He did what he wanted when he wanted.

In 1945, when Andrew was twenty-eight, he and Betsy as usual remained in Maine through the fall months, living with her mother and father at their farm, which had no telephone. A neighbor drove up in a large black car. Andy must come immediately. There was a message that he should call home. Betsy remembers Andrew listening on the phone at the neighbor's house: "He was standing all alone, as though he was seeing something that I wasn't seeing." He was seeing death. Visualizing. His sister Ann was telling him that his father—along with his grandson, Nat's three-year-old son Newell—had been hit in their car by a train at the Kuerner crossing. Both were dead.

Grim and silent as death itself, Andrew left immediately by car with Betsy for Chadds Ford. They spent the night with Betsy's sister Louise in Hartford, Connect-

icut. When Betsy awoke in the morning, Andrew was standing at the window. Crows were cawing in a nearby field. He was sobbing.

In Chadds Ford they learned the details. NC had hired Evelyn Smith, who lived beside Mother Archie's Church, to clean the schoolhouse for Andrew's arrival,

Winter 1946

Not long after his father died, Wyeth caught sight of a boy running down a hill and the image developed into this haunting tempera. It speaks of loneliness and grief. But in the gesture of the boy's hand floating in the air it suggests release and freedom.

imminent now that Halloween was near. Driving to get her, NC picked up his adored, precocious grandchild. Just before the crossing, he stopped the car and took Newell into a field where a man and woman who were building corn shocks by hand. They heard NC tell the little boy, "Newell, you won't see this again.

Remember this." Grandfather and grandson returned to the car and started forward. Then the car stopped on the track. Nobody knows why. The engineer saw the glint of sun on NC's glasses and his arm flung up, as though to ward off the train. Andrew said, "By God, it took a locomotive to kill NC Wyeth."

A month after the accident, Andrew was near the railroad crossing, struggling with a watercolor. On the broad hill across from Kuerners' appeared a boy wearing an old army jacket and leather pilot's hat. He came running, half stumbling, down the steep slope, "all topsy-turvy like a rolling stone."

The flash image of that boy, printed on Andrew's imagination, concentrated all his sorrow, the gloom that haunted every moment. The pain was even more cruel because it was love lacerated by guilt. He had shut his father out of his innermost life and art, had perhaps been unkind to this man for whom he cared so deeply, to whom he owed so much. And like his boyhood Christmases, the grief contained a thread of unthinkable gladness. He had lost his father's nurturing devotion but was also released from the pressure of NC's judgements.

The knowledge that he had to paint that sight took one second. The tempera took six months to finish and crystalized Wyeth as an artist. His father's death, like an earthquake fault, had split forever the golden, secure world he was painting in bright colors. Now his dreaming—the excitement in his associations and fantasies—was enriched by profoundly deep and anguished emotions. Releasing his terrible feelings into the tempera, he was like a drowning man, much of his life

Karl. 1948
In the plastered attic room of the Kuerner farmhouse, Karl stands beneath hooks used for hanging sausages to cure.

Overleaf: **Christina's World.** 1948
Christina Olson, Wyeth's neighbor in Maine, was painted from his imagination lying in the field below her house.

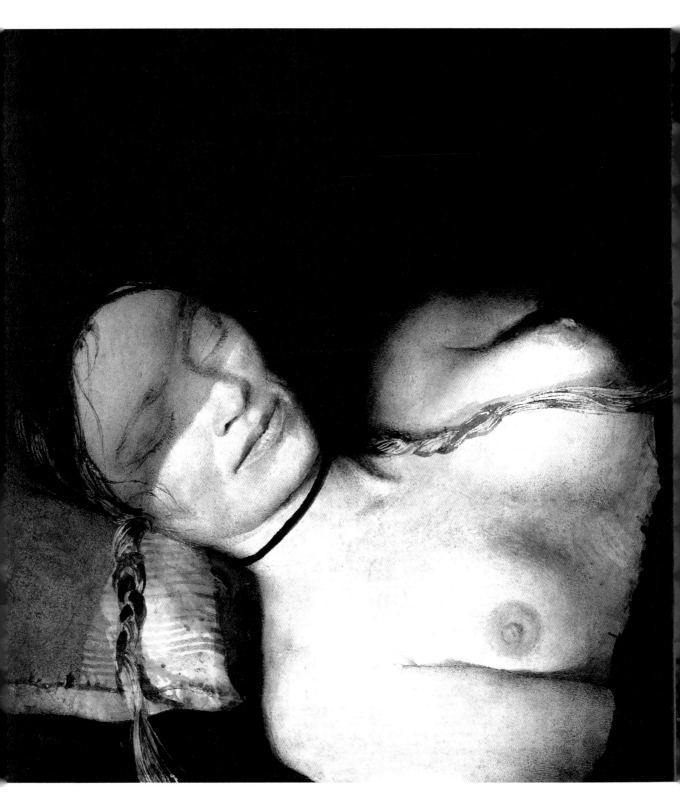

Night Shadow. 1948

passing through his dreams. And he kept hearing again the words of an ancient black woman who had told him that the train's whistle—like his father's call—had stuck and kept echoing across the little valley. She had said, "The killer's voice was blowing all morning."

The great barrel chest of the hill became his father. The boy became himself, his lost feeling of disconnection from his world. For the boy's hand, he used his own as a model. Wyeth says, "That hand was my free soul, groping. I had a terrific urge to prove that what my father had started in me wasn't in vain," Wyeth says. "I wanted to really *do* something, not just play around with it. His death lifted me out of being a clever watercolorist and into facing life, not doing caricatures of life. I saw the country even more simplified and somber, saw what the whole country meant— everything a symbol. I finally had a real *reason* to paint!"

Three winters later, permanently furious at the fact of his father's death, at himself for never painting him, Andrew did a portrait of Karl Kuerner in the attic under two brutal hooks. But in Andrew's mind, Karl was NC, both of them poetic and cruel, each a Germanic force of nature. Everything that Andrew had been came together—the fantasy and the fury, the sensitivity and single-mindedness. All his powers were now focused. He was ready for his celebrated career. That summer in Maine he did *Christina's World*, still his most famous painting.

Wyeth, using many objects and people, has continued to paint his father. NC remains a central, perhaps hourly, presence in his life. The deep and complex emotions, the unfinished business, the love and fear have persisted, never soothed, finding their way year after year into the subtext of his temperas. "My father is still alive," he says. "I feel my father all around."

NC's death became immediate thirty-four years later, when Wyeth painted Helga Testorf as a nude torso in a pool of blackness. On her lips is an inscrutable smile. Her shoulders seem oddly compressed. It is that moment when Andrew Wyeth lowered his head into the lead casket and kissed his father's forehead, and felt the waxy coldness on his lips—that moment of good-bye and beginning.

List of Illustrations

Front cover: *Faraway.* 1952.
Drybrush, 13⅝ × 20¾″. Private collection

Pages 2–3
Winter Corn. 1948.
Watercolor, 30 × 40″. Private collection

Pages 4–5
Study for Pine Baron. 1976.
Pencil sketch, 18 × 23¾″. The Wyeth Collection

Page 6
Jack Be Nimble. 1976.
Watercolor, 53 × 31½″. The Wyeth Collection

Page 8
Andrew made up as an Indian.
Photograph © by Burk Uzzle

Page 9
Wolf Moon. 1975.
Watercolor, 40⅛ × 29″. The Wyeth Collection

Pages 10–11
Her Room. 1963.
Tempera, 25½ × 48″.
Collection of the William A. Farnsworth Library
and Art Museum, Rockland, Maine

Page 12
N. C. Wyeth. *The Siege of the Round-House.*
1913.
Oil on canvas, 40 × 32″.
Collection of the Brandywine River Museum,
Chadds Ford, Pennsylvania

Page 14
The family. 1923.
The Wyeth Family Archives

Page 15
N. C. Wyeth. *Portrait of My Mother.* 1929.
Oil on canvas, 36½ × 40″. Private collection

Page 17 (top right)
N. C. Wyeth. *Andy With Fire Engine.* 1923.
Oil on canvas, 34 × 30¼″.
The Wyeth Collection
Photo courtesy The Brandywine River Museum,
Chadds Ford, Pennsylvania

Page 17 (top left)
Andrew as a child.
The Wyeth Family Archives

Page 19
Andrew dressed as Mr. Hyde.
The Wyeth Family Archives

Page 20
Spring Beauty. 1943.
Drybrush, 20 × 30″.
UNL-F.M. Hall Collection
Sheldon Memorial Art Gallery
University of Nebraska, Lincoln

Page 22
Witch's Broom. 1984.
Watercolor, 22⅛ × 30″. The Wyeth Collection

Page 23
Sunday Times. 1987.
Watercolor, 22 × 30″. The Wyeth Collection

Page 24
Indian Summer. 1970.
Tempera, 42 × 35″.
Collection of the Brandywine River Museum,
Chadds Ford, Pennsylvania

Pages 26–27
The Big Room. 1988.
Watercolor, 22½ × 30″. The Wyeth Collection

Page 29
Early watercolor drawing of World War I scene.
The Wyeth Collection

Page 30
Pine Baron. 1976.
Tempera, 31⅜ × 33¼″.
Fukushima Prefectural Museum of Art
Fukushima, Japan

Page 32
Maximillian Armor. 1941.
Ink drawing, 17 × 21″. The Wyeth Collection

Page 34
Jack and Willard. 1973.
Watercolor, 21⅜ × 29¼″.
Private collection. Photo courtesy
Coe Kerr Gallery, New York

Page 37 (top)
Maiden Voyage. 1988.
Tempera, 40 × 49″. Private collection

Page 37 (bottom)
Andrew holding a toy sailboat.
The Wyeth Family Archives

Page 38 (top left)
N. C. Wyeth in his studio.
The Wyeth Family Archives

Page 38 (top right)
Andrew in musketeer costume.
The Wyeth Family Archives

Index

Italic page numbers refer to captions and illustrations.